I0170760

Awaken Within Publications 2024

© 2024 by Awaken Within Publications

ISBN: 978-1-7328116-7-6

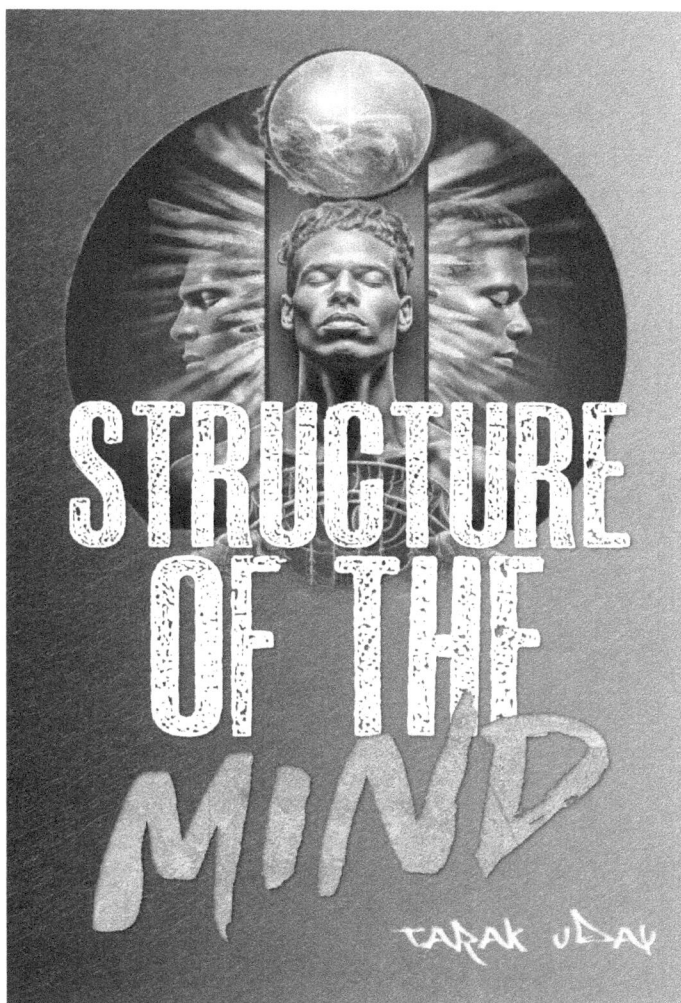

STRUCTURE OF THE MIND

TARAK UDAY

CONTENTS

INTRODUCTION

Before we begin diving into an understanding of the structure of the mind, I first want to discuss a few things. I want to call upon you to first reflect on the purpose of WHY you would want to spend time gaining further understanding of this. If we are to know and understand anything, we must first know and understand ourselves. To know who we are, how we function, we must increase our awareness of self.

The driving questions behind all knowledge seeking is "who am I?," "Where did I come from?," "Where am I going?," and "Why am I here?" Throughout this book, you should receive far greater clarity to the answer to all of these questions. At the very least, you should complete this literature with a far greater ability in discovering the answer to these questions.

The journey of self awareness and spiritual evolution comes before all other endeavors in life. All else is secondary, and all else is for the purpose of strengthening and expanding your self awareness, spiritual evolution, and soul growth.

If you find this aligns with your goals and desires then you should be excited as this book is packed with knowledge, information, techniques, and tips for deepening this for yourself as well. The purpose of this book is not for me to share what I know, or for me to gain notoriety of any kind, or to further my own authority. While all of these may end up happening, understand that the purpose of this book is for you, the reader, to benefit in a major way from having read this book.

I do not wish for you to just receive information and become fascinated with what you learn and receive. I wish for you to move forward with implementing this information into your life in a practical way to bring forth rapid transformation and expansion of your consciousness. I call upon you to create experiences for yourself in order to generate your own knowledge.

Please do not believe a single word that you read within this book. You do not want to be stuck in a faith based approach to your spiritual development. This is why I implore you to be a metaphysician and create your own experiments within your life experiences. A metaphysician is a scientist. Be a scientist and conduct your own experiments, gather your own data, do your own research, and discover your own findings. This is how you transform belief into knowledge.

The difference between believing something and knowing something is experience. I could call you on the phone right now and inform you that it is currently raining where I am located and you would likely believe me. My neighbor could call you at the same time and tell you that you are misinformed and it is actually sunny with no cloud in sight. You would be in a position where you would have to decide who to believe and who not to believe. However, if you were sitting here next to me and were to step outside and feel the raindrops on your face, there is nothing that I nor my neighbor could possibly tell you to convince you that it is not raining. This is because you would be EXPERIENCING it.

Take a moment now to reflect on your current spiritual beliefs. I would even suggest you stop for a moment, get out a pen and paper, and write these down. Make a list of everything that you believe to be true. Then follow that up with the experiences you have to support these beliefs. Take account of which beliefs have experiences associated with them, which have none at all, and which have a good amount of experiences tied to and supporting them. This will help you identify and separate which spiritual beliefs are just that, beliefs, and which ones truly are KNOWLEDGE that you have.

Sometimes it takes more than one or two experiences to fully know something. Each experience will be strengthening your belief but it will take a number of experiences to truly know that it is true. For example, let's say you are an irresponsible individual and you want to become more responsible. Having a month where you pay all of your bills before they are due may give you an experience that you have not had recently, or maybe ever before, but that would not mean that you are now a responsible individual. Your belief in your ability to become a responsible person would be greatly strengthened, but you would need to create quite a few more experiences for yourself as you continue to develop this quality within yourself. After 6 or 7 months, when this aspect is fully developed, you may then reach a point where this now strong belief in you being a responsible person crosses the threshold into KNOWING that you are now a responsible individual.

This is the Universal Law of Believing and Knowing, which is also known as the Universal Law of Manifestation. We will dive deeper into this law and ways to further use it to your benefit later on within this book.

Next I would like to talk again about your purpose for reading this book. Your purpose is your personal benefit, and the highest form of benefit is deepening the understandings we gain from the life lessons we have an opportunity to learn from what we experience in life.

Why do you want to have more self awareness? What do you want to accomplish or gain from living this life you are currently in the middle of? What brings you joy? What is your greatest obstacle right now? These are not questions you need to answer right away. They are just questions that I call upon you to contemplate and reflect on as you read this material. My personal goal for you, is to have a solid answer to these questions by the time you complete this work.

Self awareness and understanding the structure of the mind aid us in not only understanding how our mind operates, but how we create our reality. It also gives us deeper insight into our dreams and astral projection and what these experiences really are. It also deepens our awareness of who we are beyond this physical body and conscious mind we are most aware of.

CHAPTER 1

THE MIND

For many of us, when we think about who we are, we only go as far back as our birth, and only as deep as this physical body. Our existence spans lifetimes and goes so deep that just seeing the self a the physical body only would be like the entire forest thinking that it is just one leaf on a single tree. Your perspective will expand as you begin to unravel our true existence. This first chapter will set the foundation of understanding what the mind is for us to build upon later and identify how to use it for the tool that it is.

We must come to understand that our mind is far more than just chemicals being released within the brain. It is a tool for experiencing in order to know the self. The brain is physical. The mind is non-physical. Our dream experiences are an excellent example of this fact. Our dream experiences are an avenue in which we can create an experience for ourselves to know this truth.

These experience are often deemed as mere hallucinations we entertain as we sleep, however, they are far more complex than that. Dream experiences are very real, and our existence within them is no less valid life experiences than the ones we experience within our waking life. You may have already had a dream, or may have one in the coming nights, that feels more real than real life!

I challenge you to begin writing down your dreams every night and deepen your awareness of your dreams. If you do this and couple it with the ability to decode and interpret the dreams using the Universal Language of the Mind, it will eventually become undeniable that your dream experiences are real. Create an experience for yourself to discover and know this to be true, or perhaps you will find out that it is false.

For some, this is the first challenging piece of information, as they have either been told or strongly believe that dreams are a just some form of chemical reactions within the brain. This is understandable because our only way of experiencing life within this physical reality is through the 6 senses. These six senses are sight, sound, smell, taste, touch, and thought. We perceive the world around us through these senses and our brain processes the input received.

Without the transference of information through these senses, we would have no awareness of our existence within this physical reality. Therefore, it is understandable that modern science would interpret any experience beyond the physical as more brain processes for currently unknown reasons while asleep. Do not rely on belief, no matter how strong. Transform your beliefs into knowledge.

However, the mind and the brain, although often used synonymously, are two completely different entities. The brain, as we know, is the hardware processor that is at the core of all functions and control for the physical body. The mind is a tool for experiencing as well. The mind is a tool for us to use in order to know who we are. Most of us when we think about the mind we think about our thoughts. However, the mind is so much more than just thoughts.

We will soon explore the expanse of our mind which will allow you to discover for yourself just how silly it seems to compare the brain with the mind. For now, lets also tackle another misconception regarding the mind. A lot of people also use the terms unconscious and subconscious synonymously as well. This is because many people are unconscious of their subconscious mind.

Unconscious just means something you are unaware of. There is much of the conscious mind that you are conscious and aware of, and there is much of the conscious mind that you are unconscious of and unaware of. There is some of the subconscious mind that you are conscious and aware of, and there is so much more of the subconscious mind that you are unconscious and unaware of. The etymology of the word "*conscious*" means "with awareness."

As you explore and discover more of your mind, whether the conscious mind or subconscious mind, you are increasing your awareness of it. As you increase your awareness, the amount of your mind that you are unconscious to will decrease. Many of us are unconscious of many different physical, mental, and emotional processes. This is not the same for the subconscious mind as the subconscious mind controls many processes within the body including temperature, heart rate, respiration, and digestion.

We can also have intuitive thoughts, which is the power of the subconscious mind, and we are able to increase our awareness of these intuitive thoughts. For example, when you think of a friend just before they text you, or think a thought as another speaks it out loud.

We will explore in depth all aspects of the subconscious mind, it's purpose, duty, and power, and in doing so, we will decrease your unconscious awareness of this part of the mind.

CHAPTER 2

3 DIVISIONS OF MIND

There are 3 different divisions of the mind: conscious, subconscious, and superconscious mind. The conscious mind is named such because it is the mind that we are most conscious of. I say this, so that you can better understand that there is a difference between the terms conscious and unconscious; being aware of something and being unaware of something, and the difference in that reference to the conscious mind itself.

Here is a two-dimensional image to help us better understand this multidimensional structure of the mind:

LIGHT
IAM

SPIRIT - 5D		SUPERCONSCIOUS MIND
SOUL - 4D		SUBCONSCIOUS MIND
BODY - 3D		CONSCIOUS MIND

Our physical body is the vehicle that our consciousness uses within the physical three-dimensional reality and it uses the conscious mind. The soul is the vehicle that our consciousness uses within the fourth dimension and it uses the subconscious mind. And our spirit is the vehicle that our consciousness uses to traverse the fifth dimension and it uses the superconscious mind. The soul and spirit are two more things that are often interchanged synonymously that are actually two completely different things.

Just as the physical body is the vehicle that our consciousness uses to experience life within this physical reality, the soul and the spirit are also just vehicles that we use in order to experience realities that are calibrated to a much higher vibration.

Do not be mistaken, you are not your body, you are not your soul, you are not your spirit, and you are not your mind. I am sure you have heard the saying "You are not a physical being having a spiritual experience, you are a spiritual being having a physical experience." Now while this saying is beneficial to help elevate into a higher perspective for some, it is still inaccurate. You are not a physical being or a spiritual being, you are your consciousness, your intelligent awareness, having a physical, astral, and spiritual experience all at the same time with varying levels of awareness of each!

This perspective introduces us to one of the most powerful purposes that we can have for, not only lucid dreaming, but dreaming of any kind. Since our dreams are occurring within the inner levels of the subconscious mind, deepening our awareness of our dreams, and even becoming lucid within our dreams, allow us to increase our awareness in astounding ways of our existence beyond this current life within this physical body. These experiences allow us to explore and create experiences within these higher dimensions.

The three dimensions of this physical reality are height, width, and depth. We can freely move around these dimensions. We are not limited in our possibility of moving around through latitude, longitude, and altitude. However we are limited in how we experience time. We are locked into this present moment. We cannot re-experience the past, and we cannot move into the future. We are locked into this ever evolving present moment.

We are also locked into the singular space of this physical body, the vehicle we have to use in order to be able to traverse this physical reality. We cannot bi-locate and be in two places at once and we cannot expand our exist out beyond this physical body to include the house we are in and even the town or city we are in.

Our soul allows us to experience the different realities of the fourth dimension. The fourth dimension is time. Within the inner levels of the subconscious mind we are no longer limited by time. We can freely move between all of the possibilities of the past and we can freely move through the infinite possibilities within the future.

The past is just as infinite in possibilities as the future is, however, due to our experience of the reality we chose to experience for ourselves within the 'past' it is harder for us to see that we can still change the past just as easily as we can change the future. We are more attached to what has happened because we have experienced it. We will break this down to its full extent within the upcoming book "The Metaphysical Mechanics of Manifestation."

The fifth dimension is space. This is why the spirit is the vehicle used here, because there is less form within this dimension. The spirit is more of an essence than it is an actual form. We are no longer limited to a singular space within this dimension. We can expand our consciousness and experience the essence of anything within space through the fifth dimension. This is the dimension of interconnectedness.

The solid lines within the mind triangle diagram display the separation between the three divisions of the mind; conscious, subconscious, superconscious. The solid line extending beyond the triangle's border delineates that the superconscious mind is whole amongst itself and the conscious mind and subconscious mind are two halves to a whole. Through the Universal Law of Duality, the subconscious mind is the feminine, receptive mind, and the conscious mind is the masculine, aggressive mind.

The thoughts of the conscious mind display this aggressive behavior as they invade our mind whether we choose to think them or not. Especially one with an undisciplined mind, you can easily see how aggressive the conscious mind can be. The subconscious mind is more receptive and subtle. You must create space within the mind in order to *receive* the thoughts of the subconscious mind.

There is a universal truth Your Thoughts Create Your Reality. This can be found in many different holy scriptures, "*as you think, so you become,*" "*as you sow, so shall you reap,*" "*as a man thinketh in his heart, so he is,*" "*your life is shaped by your mind.*" The metaphysics behind this is through the relationship between the conscious mind and subconscious mind.

Just as the seed from a man is implanted into the womb of a woman where it fertilizes and then gestates for 40 weeks before the baby is birthed out into the world, so does the conscious mind implant the seed thought within the subconscious mind where it gestates and gains form and density until it is pushed out and birthed into this physical reality.

Just as the seed for the flower is planted into the fertile earth within the ground until it grows roots and sprouts out into the outer world above, so does the conscious mind implant the seed thought within the subconscious mind where it takes root and grows until it finally sprouts into physical manifestation.

The superconscious mind has it's own dual nature. The aggressive, masculine principle of the superconscious mind is the duty of the superconscious mind. The receptive, feminine principal of the superconscious mind is the purpose of the superconscious mind. The purpose of the superconscious mind is to hold the blueprint for our existence. We have each created this blueprint for ourselves. This blueprint holds our soul's purpose and our purpose within this lifetime.

This blueprint is our destiny. We do have free will to choose when we will fulfill the different aspects of this blueprint, however, one way or another, one lifetime or another, this blueprint we have created for ourselves will continue to be fulfilled.

Within life we are presented with opportunities to learn these different life lessons, however, we can choose to learn the lesson or run from it. If we choose to run from it, then life will recreate new experiences and new opportunities to learn the same lesson that we are destined to learn. This could come back around this lifetime, or it could emerge again within a future lifetime.

This blueprint is just like any other blueprint, it is there for reference to help guide you in ensuring that what you have designed for yourself spiritually, is what actually develops. This is no different than a blueprint on a construction job site.

Let's say there is an electrician who has been laying the electrical wires to this large building that is being developed. The first two floors are complete, and he is now on the third floor, moving along perfectly. Suddenly, he makes it to a room similar to many others he has already completed, however, this time there are some water pipes right where he thought he was supposed to place his electrical wires.

Up until now, he had understood exactly what he needed to do and thought he knew what was going on. However, now he feels lost and unsure of himself. He begins to question whether all of the work he has done thus far was even correct, or if he has been doing it wrong this entire time. He pauses for a second and decides to go back to the floor level, head over to the job site trailer, and consult with the blueprint.

Upon looking at the blueprint, he sees that everything has been done correctly, however this room as a mirrored room that requires his wires to run through the opposite wall. He is invigorated as he walks back to the job site, excited to pick up where he left off with this new level of awareness and confidence.

Often in life we find ourselves in a similar situation. We feel as though we knew what we were doing, but something in life has come up, making us feel lost and unsure of ourselves. We thought we knew where we were going in life but are not sure if we have been making the right choices. When we take a moment to go within and connect with our spirit to check the blueprint, we gain more clarity and awareness of what it is we need to be doing, and better understand the purpose of why we needed to experience what we went through.

The duty of the superconscious mind is to supply lifeforce energy in order for us to fulfill this blueprint. The superconscious mind is the mind that our spirit uses. The word spirit comes from the Greek word *spiritus* and the Latin word *spirare*, both of which translate to BREATH. This is at the root of the word INSPIRATION.

This inspiration is the aggressive quality of the superconscious mind. It is feeding you the energy needed in order to fulfill the blueprint. Have you ever had an idea pop into your mind late at night and you are suddenly no longer tired, but inspired to take action upon that idea, even though it may be one or two in the morning? This is the lifeforce energy being fed into your being from the superconscious mind.

This is also why nearly all meditation practices begin with the breath. The breath ties the soul to the body and what allows our conscious mind to unite with the superconscious mind. Connecting with your breath will allow you to connect with your spirit, thus aligning you more with the superconscious mind. This is how you can take the steps to "consulting with the blueprint."

Each of the other minds also has a duty and a purpose. With the conscious and subconscious minds being two halves to a whole, their duties and purpose's are intertwined.

The aggressive duty of the conscious mind is to create life experiences for us to learn from. Every life experience that we have, whether we see it as a positive experience, a negative experience, or a neutral experience, offers us an opportunity to learn more about ourselves, the world around us, and the universe we exist within. These life lessons provide us deeper understandings into these principals.

Many people within the last few decades have been replacing the word understanding with over-standing because of a misperception of the etymology of the word. *It* is called an understanding because it provides the foundation that your knowledge and intelligence then stands upon. It is the understanding, **NOT YOU**. *It* stands under **YOU**. Because as we build deeper and deeper understandings, we increase our knowledge and wisdom.

When we learn how to truly forgive others and even ourselves because of the experiences we have, we deepen our understanding of what forgiveness truly is. This new knowledge becomes a part of the foundation of our wisdom that we stand upon as we move through life. This leads us into the purpose of the conscious mind; to feed these understandings into the soul to be stored and become permanent.

Everything within this physical reality is temporary. If and/or when we cease to exist within our current physical body, we will not be able to take anything with us outside of the memory of the experiences we had and the understandings that we have built through the experiences that we chose to learn from. By doing so we transform these into *permanent* understandings.

This ties into the receptive purpose of the subconscious mind: to store these permanent understandings within the soul. This storehouse of wisdom is the source of our intuitive knowledge. We have the ability to tap into this storehouse of wisdom at any time. This is how some people are born into this lifetime with gifts that appear to have naturally developed. Some people are born able to lucid dream as children, are naturally highly intuitive, can astral project, or communicate with souls and entities not in physical form. It is not that these individuals were somehow selected to have special gifts and talents that others don't. It is that they put in the work in prior lifetimes to build up those strengths.

This applies to more than just special gifts and abilities. I am sure if you reflect long enough you can think about different things that you came into this lifetime naturally understanding that others may not. For example, maybe you are naturally a considerate person without thinking about it. Or perhaps you naturally are a responsible person without any need to develop that quality. The understandings that we build through the life lessons that we learn are available for us to utilize and build upon for the rest of that lifetime and on into future lifetimes.

This storehouse of wisdom is the true purpose of the subconscious mind, the mind that our soul uses. This is the end game to even existing within these physical bodies, lifetime after lifetime. After we live our lifetime and pass on, what we have added to these permanent understandings is what we carry forward with us as a soul.

The duty of the subconscious mind is to manifest the desires of the conscious mind. Our thoughts create our reality, and the thoughts of the conscious mind are then implanted into the mental level of the subconscious mind. From there they gain density, move through the astral levels, until they are pushed out into the physical reality from the emotional level and made manifest.

That would be thousands of seed thoughts being cast out into the fertile soil of the subconscious mind each and every day. This is why some people have a hard time understanding the Universal Truth of creating their reality from their thoughts. They often think just thinking a thought a time or two will make it manifest. But the subconscious mind must determine which of these thousands of thoughts to provide energy to and manifest. This will be determined by the quality and quantity of the thought.

A thought is an image. How clear of an image is the thought within your mind, compounded with how often you think the thought, will determine where it falls in line amongst the thousands of other thoughts seeking to manifest. Every thought seeks to manifest. These things are not only true for the conscious thought at the surface of our awareness, this is equally true for the thoughts and beliefs that we are unaware and unconscious of.

This is a major reason why it is important to increase your concentration, your ability to control your attention. The more control you have over your attention the easier it will be to observe deeper and deeper thoughts and beliefs that you are unaware of and unconscious of.

There is another Universal Truth, *Energy Flows Where The Attention Goes.* The more attention you give to a particular thought, the more energy you feed into, the more you ensure it's manifested destiny.

CHAPTER 3

7 LEVELS OF MIND

There are 7 levels of mind within the 3 divisions of the conscious, subconscious, and superconscious mind. The seventh level is the one we are mostly familiar with. It is the physical level of mind experienced through the physical body within this 3 dimensional reality. It is the only level within the conscious mind.

The subconscious mind has four different levels: the mental level, the upper astral level, the lower astral level, and the emotional level of mind. The emotional level is the first level within the subconscious mind. This is why we call our emotions feelings, because we can *feel* our emotions.

Ninety-nine percent of all dreams occur within one of these four levels of the subconscious mind. The majority of those dreams occur within the lower and upper astral levels for most people. Dreams within the emotional level will be in black and white. Dreams within the lower astral level will be in regular technicolor. Dreams within the upper astral will be vibrant, striking colors. Dreams within the mental level will have virtually no color, more of a heavenly feel.

LIGHT
I AM

SPIRIT - 5D	1ST LEVEL — COSMIC CONSCIOUSNESS	SUPERCONSCIOUS MIND
	2ND LEVEL — CAUSAL	
	3RD LEVEL — MENTAL	
SOUL - 4D	4TH LEVEL — UPPER ASTRAL	SUBCONSCIOUS MIND
	5TH LEVEL — LOWER ASTRAL	
	6TH LEVEL — EMOTIONAL	
BODY - 3D	7TH LEVEL — PHYSICAL	CONSCIOUS MIND

Between the upper and lower astral levels is where you can locate the akashic records. Akasha is a Sanskrit word meaning *"the all."* The akashic records are library of all vibrations that have ever reverberated. With the fourth dimension being free of the limitation of time, one could experience every past life they ever lived, the history of the world or universe, or any conceivable question their mind could generate.

Through our dreams within the fourth dimension we can also perceive any and all possible and probable timelines. People have started talking about "jumping timelines" as if there are an infinite number of you's living an infinite number of lives within an infinite number of timelines. In actuality, a more proper perspective is to see that here in the physical you still only have this singular present moment.

Through working with the subconscious mind one has the possibility of transforming this present moment into an infinite number of possibilities. You can change the past just as simply as you can change the future. It may be more difficult because you are likely more attached to the "past" that you have experienced which is heavily influencing what you are creating for yourself in this present moment reality. You must continually let go of your background and your past. Allow yourself to be open to transforming into any state of being that you want to exist within. The more your present reality differs from your desired reality, the more you need to be able to let go of your past, what you have experienced, and who you were.

The mental level is where thoughts are formed. When a thought becomes strong enough within the conscious mind it is imprinted into the mental level where a new, identical thought is formed.

Our thoughts are less dense than our emotions or the energy of the astral, so they are less perceivable. This is also reflected in the elemental quality of the third level of mind. The elemental quality of the mental level is air. The upper astral level is slightly more dense and has an elemental quality of fire. The elemental quality of the lower astral is water, and the elemental quality of the emotional level is the earth element.

This can be found encoded into many different holy scriptures and ancient stories as well. I once had a dream where I was on the roof of a skyscraper [superconscious dream symbol] with my mother [superconscious dream symbol] and sister. I immediately ran over and jumped off of the roof.

After falling only five or ten feet I entered a void momentarily and then cam out of the void and was falling thorough an endless sky. Just as I was really enjoying this freeing free fall I entered another void. When I came out of the void I was falling through the air still but this time I could see the earth down below. As far as my eye could see the entire earth was filled with bursting volcanoes and flowing rivers of lava.

I went back into another void and came out to a new realm where the entire earth was completely covered in water. As far as the eye could see you could only see water. Every time I was closer and closer to the ground. I re-entered another void and emerged just a thousand feet above an endless, lush forest. Just as I reached the canopy top I woke up.

I had been presented this information of the elemental qualities of the 4 levels of the subconscious mind the same as you have now. I have also studied its presence within different holy scriptures and ancient stories as this knowledge is ancient and not new. But it wasn't until this dream experience that I had experienced it for myself. This was no regular dream either, the moment I crested the edge of the rooftop I became lucid. I can still to this day see the images just as vivid as when it happened, and can recall the feeling of the air rushing across my face.

With more experiences, this belief would deepen into knowledge. These are elemental qualities of these levels of mind because each element as we know them are physical things. Even air, being the most difficult to perceive, can still be experienced and perceived by the senses as a physical thing. However, each of these four levels of the inner subconscious mind are beyond the physical. They are our first experiences of the non physical. So each of these elements help us to understand the QUALITY of the energy of these levels.

The quality of the mental level is that of air. We can not see the air; it is hard to perceive, but if we give it our full attention, we can sense it's presence. Our thoughts are the same way. Even though they are constantly in play and such a prevalent part of our existence, we only sense their presence when we truly place out attention upon them.

The air is also easily influenced and can be moved and swayed. The same is true for the chitta [mind substance] of the mental level. It is easily moldable and simple to alter. The quality of the energy of this level is motion. When we first implant a new seed thought into the mental level it is easy for it to change and shift into anything we want. It is also easily affected by new thoughts.

The elemental quality of the upper astral is fire. The element of fire is expansive. That is the energy of the upper astral, the mind substance here is very expansive. Once a thought makes it into this level of mind it is like a wild fire expanding out into a million different possibilities and ways that it could manifest. When a thought is here within the mind the Universal Law of Infinity is truly at play.

Fire, like air, is not very dense and is free-flowing. However it needs something to attach to, it needs a source of fuel, it is not quite as free flowing as the element of air. As you seed thought idea makes it into this level you want to continue imaging the end result that you are desiring and not limit the universe in HOW you are wanting it to manifest.

The elemental quality of the lower astral level is water. Water is more dense than air and fire but still more free flowing than the earth element. Swimming through water is far easier than through dirt or mud, but nowhere near as free as moving through the air.

The energy of this level is contraction. After passing through the infinite possibilities of manifestation, when a thought form makes it down into the lower astral, It begins to contract into a more finite number of possibilities. Just as other liquids can influence water and change its chemical structure, so too can a thought form still be influenced by new thoughts.

The elemental quality of the emotional level is earth. We can feel our emotions. We can really tell that they are there and that they exist. It is easier to perceive our emotions than it is our thoughts just as it is easier to perceive and feel the ground beneath your feet than it is the air all around.

The energy of the chitta within this level of the subconscious mind is stability. Just like a healthy baby just before birth, the thought forms here are fully developed and ready to make their way into the physical reality. The number four represents stability, and as this is the fourth level that our thought form has now moved into within the subconscious mind, it has gained stability and is ready to manifest.

Emotions in our life are like road signs. They are reflecting to us, and giving us insight into what is manifesting or has just recently manifested within our reality. Remember, our thoughts create our reality. Whenever we experience a 'positive' emotion, it is because something we are desiring is manifesting or has manifested. Whenever we experience a 'negative' feeling, it is because something we do not want is manifesting or has manifested.

Thus, use your emotions as you would street signs on the side of the road. When we are on a long journey we rely on the road signs to know when we are going to fast and need to slow down, to tell us when we need to change lanes and get off at the next exit and change into a new direction. When we elevate our perspective on our emotions and see them in this new way, it becomes easier to not remain attached to the emotions.

Freeing ourselves from the grip of anger, sadness, jealousy, fear, worry, or anxiety makes it easier to RESPOND to life's situations and circumstances, rather than simply REACTING to them. This is the true essence of the word *responsibility*; your ABILITY to RESPOND!

A thought is an image. To give yourself an experience to begin to move from having to rely on believing this into knowing it is true I want you to think of a balloon. Just pause and take a moment right now to think about a balloon. Now say out loud the color the balloon you saw. You could not only say the color of the balloon, but you could also describe if it was a black background or the sky was the background, or maybe it had a sting on it, or it was tied to a stick.

You can describe the thought of the balloon because the thought was an image. All our thoughts are images. It may take more work and effort for you to increase your awareness of this truth, but that still doesn't make it any less true.

It is important for you to understand this in order to know the deeper purpose to decoding your dreams. When you understand every thought is an image, and you understand how a thought moves through the different levels of the subconscious mind, along with the understanding that our dreams occur within the subconscious mind, then we can then make our way to understanding that the images within our dream are just the thoughts that we have within the subconscious mind.

This is one of the greatest values within, not just lucid dreaming, but dream recall in general. The more aware you are of your dreams and the deeper your dream experiences, the more your self awareness increases. Another benefit is that with lucid dreaming, you can help move the thoughts along that you do want to manifest, or change and transform the thoughts that you do not want to manifest.

There are two different levels within the superconscious mind. The causal level of the superconscious mind and the first level of mind, which is cosmic consciousness; also known as Christ consciousness or Buddha consciousness. The fifth dimension has no limitation on space. This is why the quality of the superconscious mind is interconnectedness.

Take another moment to examine the mind diagram:

A triangle is the perfect shape to convey our experience through these different levels of the mind. When our everyday perspective is within the conscious mind in this physical reality, the two sides seem so far apart and separate. This is why when we look around in our outer world we see everything as separate from ourselves. The deeper into the mind that we go, the closer and closer that the two sides appear. Once we reach the top of the superconscious mind, we can see that there was never a left side and a right side, but just one border creating the whole shape. This is reflective of the elevated perspective that the superconscious mind provides, we can see the true nature of reality, which is interconnectedness and the illusion of separation fades away.

This is why Jesus Christ and Gautama Siddhartha the Buddha focused so much on loving others, taking care of your fellow man, and seeing yourself in all other things and beings within all of nature. When we move into superconscious mind this is not a concept but a growing awareness of our true reality. It becomes an existence, because it truly is. This expansive awareness provides us with a more elevated view. Our physical life within this one lifetime is no longer subject, seen from in the midst of it all. It can now be viewed objectively where the whole picture can be brought into view.

This expansive perspective is what is needed to be able to have the full blueprint for our existence within all of the other levels of mind. Thought is cause. The thoughts of this blueprint, and the lifeforce energy they are charged with are sent out from the causal level of mind.

CHAPTER 4

THE POWERS OF THE MIND

All three divisions of mind are unique in location, operation, as well as ability and opportunity. Because of their own unique mechanics, they each provide a unique power and ability for us to utilize. The conscious mind is the division of mind that we are most familiar with. The power of the conscious mind will also be the one that we are most familiar with and more easily identify compared to the others.

The power of the conscious mind is reasoning. The three keys of reasoning are memory, attention, and imagination. Our memory allows us to better understand what we experienced in the past. Our attention allows us to better understand what we are experiencing in the present moment. And our imagination allows us to better understand what we have the opportunity to experience in the future.

Each of these mental skills can be strengthened and controlled. Each of these mental skills is like mental muscles and just like our physical muscles it takes regular exercise and discipline in order to strengthen them. If you are not regularly spending time and energy to build these mental skills, they are growing weaker by the day.

Concentration is your ability to control your attention. Visualization is your ability to control your imagination. Now that we better know and understand the duty and purpose of the conscious mind, and its relationship with the subconscious mind, we can understand how this power of reasoning can be best utilized to fulfill that purpose and complete that duty.

Improving your memory is helpful, improving your visualization is powerful, but increasing your power of concentration is vital, ESPECIALLY if we are talking about lucid dreaming. There is another Universal Truth, *You are Where Your Attention is.* This is especially evident when you are lucid dreaming or astral projecting. Your attention is going to determine where you go, what you manifest, and what you experience within the astral realm as you are lucid dreaming and astral projecting. If you have no control over your attention, then you will have no control of where you go, what you see, and what you experience within any lucid dream or out of body experience.

The same is true for your waking life as well. Remember, your dreams are a direct reflection of how you use your mind while awake. If you are unable to control where your attention is throughout the day, then you will forever remain a slave to the wild direction that your thoughts lead you in.

Have you ever had an experience of someone telling you a story or trying to get your attention but you were day dreaming or lost in thought and unable to recall any of what they said. You were no longer present in that room, but lost in your mind wherever your attention led you. Even though your ears may have physically heard the words of the individual speaking to you, you didn't actually hear any of it because your attention was on your thoughts. Thus, you were where your attention was, as it is universally true: *You Are Where Your Attention Is.*

By spending 5 minutes a day each on memory, concentration exercises, and visualization practices, you can truly transform yourself and your life.

MEMORY EXERCISE

To increase the power of your memory, I suggest practicing the 5-day 5-step exercise. This is a memory exercise that will exponentially increase the power of your memory. The 5-day 5-steps exercise is recalling, in reverse order, five moments throughout your day, for 5 days straight.

First, recall an event you were just doing, such as eating dinner. Pull to mind a clear image of the experience. It does not need to be in full detail, but be sure to see the who, what, where of the experience.

Then you want to call to mind a mental snapshot of what you were doing just before the first experience, possibly leaving work and headed home. Next, you will recall your experience prior to the second one, perhaps a meeting with your boss. You will then want to pull to mind a snapshot of what you were doing before the third experience, maybe you had lunch at your favorite restaurant. Lastly, you will call to mind an image of what you did early in the day, something like brushing your teeth

*as you were preparing for the day,
or making breakfast for yourself.*

*You only need to call to mind who
all was there and what you were
doing; a quick snapshot is
sufficient, there is no need to recall
full details of the whole experience.
You have now completed 5
steps, or moments, within 1 day.
Like opening a drawer in a file
cabinet, you pulled out and
glanced at five files within this first
drawer.*

*Now, do the same for the four
previous days, starting with the
end of the day and working your
way in reverse order to the
beginning of the day. You will also
want to make sure to space things
out. You don't want all 5 of your
memories clumped up at the end of
the day, or in the beginning. If that
has to happen for a day or two that
is totally fine, there are no
absolutes with this exercise, no
right or wrong to be bothered with,
I am only guiding you through the
most optimal way to perform the
exercise.*

*Once you recall 5 steps for 5 days,
starting with the end of the day
moving to the beginning, you will
have completed the exercise.*

You will want to practice this EVERY. SINGLE. DAY. It may be difficult at first, possibly taking five to ten minutes for your first few days. That is OK; the more you practice, the easier and quicker it will become to complete this exercise.

Our memory is a mental muscle. The more we work it out and exercise it, the stronger it will become. With this in mind, be sure to take your time with it. It is similar to having a desire to begin working out and you don't normally work out or haven't done it for years. Just starting out like that you wouldn't walk into the gym and try to bench press 275 lbs and squat 450lbs on day 1, would you? I certainly don't think so.

You would likely start with benching something light to get the muscles moving, squatting just 100 plus pounds, maybe 200. However, eventually, with hard work and dedication, you would likely find yourself lifting heavier amounts and achieving more repetitions. This memory exercise is no different. Eventually, you may be able to complete this exercise in 30 or 40 seconds. Anything under a minute would be ideal. However, you have to start somewhere and take small steps from there.

To help you out in the beginning you may find it easier to write the moments down so that you can have assistance in recalling the memories. You can write down each of the 5 moments of all 5 days. Then you can refer to your list, review the day's events, and pull them to mind as you go back through the last 5 days. This is an excellent way to get things started for the first week or two.

Eventually you will want to ween yourself off of the written aid. It is a great way to ease into things, especially if it's been a long time since you had to exercise your memory but we do not want to rely upon it for too long or we may hinder our growth. If you do write the 5 things down for 5 days make sure you don't go longer than 2 weeks before you begin to transition to not needing any written reminders for assistance.

A great way to transition is to go from 5 days of written notes to just 4 days. At this first phase of the transition, you would recall all 5 of today's experiences without the assistance of any written notes and then use the notes for the previous four days. After 2 or three days [or even 1 week], move on to recalling 2 days from pure memory and using notes to aid you with the last 3 days. Then transition to 3 days from pure memory and only two days of notes.

Keep this up, only spending 1 or 2 days [a week at the most], on each level until you finally make it to doing the exercise every day without any written assistance. If you're still struggling, consider taking pictures with your phone throughout the day and adding them to your notes. Then wean yourself off using the same pattern, starting with 1 day with only notes and 4 days with notes and pictures, until you reach 5 days of only notes. Then you can work on weening yourself off the notes.

CONCENTRATION EXERCISE

If you want to increase the power of your concentration, I suggest you practice the candle concentration exercise. This concentration exercise will exponentially increase your power over your attention. The candle concentration exercise is an exercise where you will practice giving a command to your attention, placing it somewhere specific, and then using your will power to hold it there.

Here is what you will want to do. Gather a candle, a pencil, and a piece of paper. If you have the ability to use a timer outside of your phone, like a kitchen timer, that would be ideal. If you must use your phone, ensure it's in airplane mode prior to starting the exercise. You will want to give this exercise your full attention.

You will want to sit at a table for this exercise as well. The candle should be at a height where the flame is eye level so that you do not need to bend your neck in order to look at the flame. Ideally, you will have a candle stick or maybe place the candle onto a stack of books.

When you're ready, set your timer. 10 minutes is best when starting out, but if that seems like too much for you to start out with, then begin with 5 minutes and work your way up. With your timer set and your candle positioned at eye level, about an arms length away, you will want to prepare your paper.

Remember, we are metaphysicians and want to be scientists with everything that we do. We will want to document everything. Begin by writing the date and time. Next you will light your candle and start your timer.

Once you begin the exercise, start by placing your attention on the flame of the candle and hold it there. This is all we are doing for this exercise. We are commanding our attention to go where we want it to be, and then we are using our will power to hold it there. When you notice your attention has shifted away from the flame of the candle, make a tic mark on your page with your pencil. This is making a physical acknowledgment that you are distracted.

After making a tic mark, take a deep breath, refocus your attention on the flame, and hold it there for as long as possible. You will continue this cycle of realizing when you become distracted, placing a tic mark, taking a breath, bringing your attention back, holding it there, distraction, tic mark, breath, flame, hold, distraction.....

When you make your tic mark there is no need to take your eyes off of the flame. You should keep your eyes fixed on the flame. Make your tic mark, lift your pencil, and place it in position to make the next tic mark when you become distracted again.

You could find yourself distracted by a sound, or an itch suddenly on your shoulder or even a thought. A thought of "Am I doing this right?" *is a distraction. A thought of* "I need to make my grocery list after this," *is a distraction. Even a thought of* "Flame, flame, flame, flame..." *is a distraction. If your attention is on your thoughts, then it is not on the flame.*

Once the timer goes off and the exercise is complete, tally up the total number of tic marks, write this number below them, and circle it. Then draw a line under the paper to separate today's entry and leave an open space for tomorrows entry.

This exercise is just like working out your physical muscles, the more reps you do the more you will be building and strengthening the muscles of the body. The more reps you get directing your attention on where to go and holding it there, the faster and stronger your concentration power will grow.

VISUALIZATION EXERCISE
To increase your power of visualization, I suggest you practice the 'Top 10 Most Wanted List'. This is a manifestation exercise that has a powerful visualization component with it that will exponentially increase your power over your imagination. Begin by compiling a list of the 10 desires you currently want the most. This can be a mix of physical possessions, goals, experiences, and qualities.
The list should have at least one or two desires that can be manifested within 2 or 3 weeks.

One big goal with this list is to build success consciousness. For *larger, long-term goals like having a million dollars, finishing school, buying a house, or starting a family, especially if you're currently making $50k a year, not enrolled in school, single, and renting, break these goals down into smaller steps. Break down what is the first step of these larger goals, and write that down.*

For example, if you make $50k a year with $3,000 in savings, your first goal might be to save $10,000, then $25k, and so on. If your goal is to finish school and you haven't enrolled yet, start by choosing a school to attend, enrolling in classes, and deciding on a major. If you want to buy a house but are currently renting, instead of simply writing 'own a home', start by saving for the down payment and closing costs, then work on paying off your credit cards and loans, and then aim to improve your credit score by 25 points.

These larger desires can be broken down into smaller steps, and when you manifest one you can cross it off and write down the next step, working your way to the larger end result. This helps to build success consciousness as you rapidly start knocking out all of the steps towards your larger goal. This is a much better approach than if you had a list of 10 long term items that after 4 months you didn't seem to be having any success in manifesting.

Once you have your top ten desires, order them from most important [1] to the 10th most important [10]. After ordering them, your list is complete. Start working on the list immediately. Don't wait to make the perfect list; it's meant to be temporary. If your list has remained unchanged after a month, you are doing something wrong and need to either reconsider your goals, or change how you are spending your energy throughout the day.

After completing your list, begin the visualization portion of the exercise. Every morning and every night you will want to read your list from number 1 down to number 10. Once you read #1, close your eyes and fully visualize what you want to manifest. Focus on creating the end result. Don't worry about HOW it will manifest and show up in your life, focus on the end result.

Visualization is far more than just creating the visual image. Fully immerse yourself into this visualized image. This means seeing it, smelling it, hearing it, tasting it, and FEELING it! Fully immerse yourself into this image with all of the senses of your inner mind.

This should not be a still image. This should be a moving image within your mind. To assist with this, imagine what the you, living in this manifested reality, are truly like. How do they think? What habits do they have? What do they do with their day, how do they start their day? How do they interact and communicate with other people? How do they approach problems that arise and how do they go about finding solutions?

This is crucial because you're not just manifesting these things, experiences, or goals; you are BECOMING them! You are moving into the state of being that exists within this manifested reality. This is why full immersion into that version of you is essential. The better you can be at creating this new state of being, the better you will be at manifesting these alternate realities.

After fully visualizing #1, move on to #2, and continue doing this visualization exercise with every single desire on the list. Again, repeat this process every single morning and every single night. Another great benefit that this provides is that it helps you to identify how you are spending your energy. Doing this exercise in the morning helps you set up your day to ensure you're actively working towards at least one of these desires. When you do the exercise at the end of the day, it provides you the opportunity to accurately and honestly assess how well you did at doing activities and feeding energy into any of these desires.

This is valuable insight because when you go through an entire day and realize you provided no energy towards these desires, and conducted zero activity to manifesting any of them, then this means one of two things: [1] either you mismanaged how you spent your time and energy throughout the day that day, or [2] some of these items are not truly among your top ten most wanted desires.

If you find that there is something on the list that needs to come off, or that there is something not on there that you need to place on there, you can simply rearrange the list and make a new list. One of the biggest factors with this exercise is the full immersion, using all of your inner senses to experience the end result.

If you have a desire on your list where you have $10,000 saved in the bank as extra capital then you may want to assess, how much cash does that version of me walk around with in their pocket at all times. Perhaps you decide that individual always carries $500. This helps discover the habits and way of thinking of your evolved self.

Visualize looking into your wallet or purse and seeing 5 crispy Benjamin Franklins or a large stack of twenties. Feel you hand reaching down into your pocket and holding onto the roll of cash, rubbing on the bills and really feeling the texture of the bills. Smell the unique smell of money. Experience the excitement of walking into a store, knowing you *can buy ANY item that is inside. Hear the teller announce your new balance as you deposit another $2000 into your account. Be creative and use your imagination to fully immerse yourself into these moving images.*

One more thing I want to mention has to do with other people in your visualized images. You do not want to impose your will upon the will of other specific people. Never include specific people into your visualizations. If you desire a new relationship, then be sure to just image a person holding the qualities that you want to see in your partner, do not visualize your crush and try to manifest a relationship with them. If it ends up being them, then great, but if you use your metaphysical skills and knowledge to force an experience upon someone else for your own selfish desires, you will be incurring karma that you do not want and it will likely create more problems than solutions.

Now if you already have a relationship with someone, feel free to visualize and work to manifest the desired reality that you both want. For example, if you and your partner have a common goal that you are desiring together, it is suggested to include them in your visualizations. If you are looking for a promotion at work, or a better relationship with your boss or one of your coworkers, that is OK to include them into your visualized images because these are things that the desire as well.

Summary of exercises

<u>MEMORY</u>
- *Recall 5 moments of the day in reverse order*
- *Recall 5 moments of the day in reverse order from the previous 4 days as well*
- *Complete all 25 moments in reverse order once a day every day*

<u>CONCENTRATION</u>
- *Gather a candle, pencil, paper, and timer*
- *Set your timer for 10 minutes*
- *Light your candle*
- *Write down the date and time on to the paper*
- *Start your timer*
- *Place your attention on the flame.*

- *Make a tic mark on your page when you realize your attention is anywhere other than the flame*
- *Place your attention back on the flame and use your will power to hold it there*
- *Repeat until the ten minutes is up*

VISUALIZATION

- *Write down the top ten desires that you want most in life right now*
- *Place the desires in order from number one being the most wanted and number ten being the tenth most wanted*
- *Read the list one at a time and visualize in full detail the manifestation of the desire; the end result*
- *Read this list at least once a day [ideally you will read it 3 times a day]*

Regular practice and discipline strengthening of these three mental skills will transform your life. If you do not become the master of your mind, then you will always remain a slave to it. Your thoughts create your reality. Your memory, concentration, and visualization powers will determine your ability to CHOOSE which thoughts your mind produces. This is what gives you control over the experiences you have within this physical reality, as well as the person you evolve into.

Reasoning is the power of the conscious mind. The power of the subconscious mind is intuition. Your intuition is your direct grasp of truth; your ability to perceive the truth without having any reason to be able to know. This is due to the combined qualities of: the subconscious mind being free of the limitation of time, the storehouse of wisdom we hold from the understandings we deepen through our life experiences, our connection to the akashic records, as well as the subconscious mind being our access into universal mind.

Universal mind is the way in which all of our minds are interconnected. We have all had numerous experiences where we are thinking of someone and they call or text us. Or a time when we are thinking of a song in our head, and then we hear someone start singing it out loud, or we turn on the radio and it's playing.

Intuition is also a byproduct of one's mental perception. In all of the instances we just discussed it is merely a matter of perceiving something with your inner mind, versus with your outer senses of the physical body. The etymology of the word 'intuition' comes from the Latin word *'intuicion,'* which means 'to look at.' Just as our physical body has senses to perceive our outer environment, our astral body has senses to be able to perceive our inner environment. The greater our ability to perceive through these senses with awareness in our conscious mind, the greater our intuition is.

The 6 senses of the physical body are sight, sound, touch, smell, taste, and thought. *Clairvoyance* is your ability to perceive your astral sense of sight. *Clairaudience* is your ability to perceive your astral sense of sound. *Clairsentience* is your ability to perceive your astral sense of touch. *Clairalience* is your ability to perceive your astral sense of smell. *Clairsgustance* is your ability to perceive your astral sense of taste. *Claircognizance* is your ability to perceive your astral sense of thought.

Even though you may be in your living room, can you perceive within your mind the smell of the elephant house in the zoo? Can you recall the smell of soap? Can you recall the smell of a skunk? These scents that you are perceiving are not coming through your physical nose. This is your clairalience ability of perceiving smells through your astral senses. Some will say, 'that is just your memory of a past experience of you smelling this before!' And they are absolutely correct! Remember, the subconscious mind is free from time. Your astral body is moving through time and re-smelling that scent for you.

These are the senses you will want to activate, use, and strengthen within the immersion of the visualization exercise. The more powerful that we can build up these inner senses, the more powerful our intuition will become. The more familiar that we can become with these inner senses, the more comfortable we will be within our inner projections through lucid dreaming, when we are experiencing the inner levels of the subconscious mind *through* these senses.

The power of the conscious mind is reasoning. The power of the subconscious mind is intuition, and the power of the superconscious mind is awareness. More accurately it can be described as transcendence. The superconscious mind is the deepest part of the mind. It is free from the limitations of time and space. This allows the thoughts of the superconscious mind to be aware of all of time and all of space. This is expanded awareness in its truest form. This allows for an elevated perspective in comparison to the conscious and subconscious minds. The higher perspective allows us to transcend our previous level of awareness and overcome any obstacles that may have been in our way.

When we are able to align the conscious and subconscious minds together, we then have the opportunity to harmonize them with the superconscious mind. This is the key to transcending our consciousness. The master teachers throughout history were able to do this, thus their words and teachings had a transcendent effect due to the elevated awareness their consciousness was operating from. This is the ultimate blueprint we all hold for ourselves within the superconscious mind. Just as every acorn, whether it takes root or not, whether it sprouts and grows or not, still holds that blueprint for a giant oak tree within it.

Continue to reflect, contemplate, and incorporate this information into your life. Through creating experiences for yourself, you can transform this information into your own knowledge of the true structure of your mind. This understanding is important for you to be able to move into lucid dreaming with the highest purpose possible, to increase your self awareness through navigating the inner levels of the mind with conscious awareness.

CHAPTER 5

THE REAL SELF

We have talked about the physical body, the soul, the spirit, the conscious mind, the subconscious mind, and the superconscious mind. However, you are not any of these. Many people only identify with the physical body because they do not concern themselves with or have any awareness of anything deeper. Some people identify their true selves as one of the vehicles used to experience a higher dimension, such as the soul or spirit, because they have an awareness of something beyond the physical but it is only surface level and the deepest they get is understanding they exist beyond the physical body.

LIGHT I AM

SPIRIT - 5D — SUPERCONSCIOUS MIND

SOUL - 4D — SUBCONSCIOUS MIND

BODY - 3D — CONSCIOUS MIND

You then have others who are aware of an existence outside of the body. However, many of these people use the spirit and soul synonymously because they know of no difference, or even think incorrectly that the soul is deeper than the spirit. This is usually because, even though they may have experienced themselves outside of their body, they were told these other things and have believed them, without creating enough experiences of their own to come to KNOW what is true.

Those who continue to dive deeper into themselves will discover that their true nature, their Real Self is their consciousness that merely uses these bodies and minds as tools for experiencing life in order for us to truly know and understand ourselves. Our consciousness is our own individual ray of light of the creator... our true Divine Intelligence. Continue to press on in your soul growth and spiritual development until you begin to create experiences for yourself to know this as your reality for yourself.

This knowledge has been preserved within many holy scriptures. In the bible God says, 'I AM that I AM.' There is a reason that the phrase I AM is used. Even in Psalm 82:6, the bible states, 'Ye are Gods, divine beings of The Most High.' Your I AM is your own individual ray of the Creators light. This is your consciousness. Your Real Self, your True Self. In the Bhagavad Gita Lord Krishna says in chapter 10 verse 20, "I AM the Self."

The Yogi Sutras of Patanjali are the most straightforward in saying, 'Yoga is the cessation of the movements of the mind. Then the seer abides in his own true nature.' Yoga means union. The union aspired for is a union with the Real Self our IAM divine consciousness.

Most people only know yoga as the stretching that people do in yoga studios here in America. This is Raja Yoga, one of the four yogas that are engineered to align the outer self with the inner self to then unite with the Real Self. Raja Yoga is also meditation, breathe work, and the other exercises mentioned earlier in this book.

There are three other yogas in addition to Raja Yoga. Karma Yoga is the focus upon your actions and intentions. It is important to align your intentions with those of the True Self and perform the actions that harmonize with that.

Bhakti Yoga is the yoga of devotion. Being devoted to the ideals of the Real Self. This is traditionally expressed through prayer and chanting and similar practices. But when you understand the metaphysics of both prayer and chanting, you realize that these practices are ways to program and reprogram your mind to remain devoted to the ideals of the True Self.

The fourth yoga is Jnana Yoga, the yoga of knowledge. This is practiced through contemplation to elevate your perspective. This is also practiced through increasing self awareness through dream interpretation and practically applying metaphysical and spiritual concepts into your life to generate your own knowledge. It is also practiced by fulfilling the purpose of the conscious and subconscious minds through learning the life lessons available to us within our life experiences.

These activities will produce a great many things for you within your life and transform who you are. However, it is key to remember that the true purpose is YOGA – union with the Real Self, your I AM, our Divine Consciousness. The scripture says, 'Yoga is the cessation of the movements of the mind. Then the seer abides in his own true nature.' When you are able to still the mind through any of these practices within the four yogas, then you will unify with your true nature.

There is another scripture within the Yogi Sutras of Patanjali that also reiterates for us that our I AM is beyond the mind, saying, 'The higher consciousness is beyond the vastness and minuteness; it is unborn, bright, and beyond the mind.' It is beyond the mind, it is a part of the creators light. When it says, *'it beyond the vastness and the minuteness'* it sounds contradictory. However, the vastness and minuteness indicate size; they indicate a measurement of form. However, our I AM, our Real Self, is beyond the three dimensions of our physical reality. It is beyond the dimension of time and it is beyond the dimension of space. It is outside of time and space. It has no form. It is unborn, it has no beginning, this is our connection to The Most High, the Divine Creator, the Infinite Intelligence,

Infinite Being, Infinite Energy, and Infinite Manifestation.

Everything within this book, any material I provide, and anything that I share and teach is with the ultimate purpose of aiding you in aligning with your own divine consciousness. This is why I always encourage you to never believe anything that I say, but instead to find ways to implement it into your life. In this way you will create your own experiences and through these experiences you are able to transform your beliefs into knowledge.

CHAPTER 6

ANCIENT KNOWLEDGE

The information within this book is not new in any way. It is ancient knowledge passed down for thousands of years. You just have to have 'eyes to see and ears to hear.' It also helps if you know how to decipher and decode this hidden knowledge.

For anyone who has read my first book Life is but a Dream: Understanding Your Self Through Understanding Your Dreams, then you are well aware of the language that our mind communicates in. This knowledge is invaluable as it provides insight to how your inner subconscious mind is communicating to you through your dreams. These nightly messages are personal, accurate, and direct reflections of what is occurring within your mind. This clarity can give invaluable insight into how to overcome obstacles, manifest desires, and transform negative unproductive aspects of the self and personal limiting beliefs.

This language holds just as much value for a seeker of knowledge and truth in its ability to decode the hidden gems within the holy scripture of all cultures. Some scriptures, such as the Tao Te Ching, Dhamapadda, and the Yogi Sutras of Patanjali were written at a time and within a region where the ancient knowledge being passed down did not need to be hidden due to persecution and societal control from the ruling systems. Due to this they can be more straightforward and direct in the knowledge and truth that is conveyed within those works.

The bible was written at a time and within a region where the metaphysical concepts and gems needed to be encoded within the text. This was necessary to ensure that this ancient knowledge made it through the Kali Yuga for us to benefit from today and moving forward for our own spiritual evolution.

The Kali Yuga was a time period spanning from 700 BC until 1700 AD. Our solar system spirals around the sun, as the sun spirals around another star deeper into the galaxy. Just as we cycle through the seasons each orbit around the sun, the yugas are the 'seasons' that we move through as we get closer and further from the center of the galaxy. The Kali yuga is almost like the 'winter' of this larger orbit, as it is a time of limited energy and prana available on this planet as it is the portion of this cycle that is furthest away from the center of the Milky Way.

In the year 500 AD we were at the furthest point from the center of the galaxy and no longer were getting further and further away, and began our shift getting closer and closer to the center of the galaxy. Prior to that, for the previous 12,000 years there was less and less energy available on the planet with each passing day. Ever since then, there is more and more energy each day than there was the day before and that will continue for the next 10,500 years. This time period in the east is known as the dark ages, spanning from 500 AD to 1500 AD.

The bible was written with deep symbolism within the Universal Language of the Mind in order to transfer this knowledge through the darkest times our civilizations here on Earth have faced within the Kali yuga. When we decode the first 10 versus of the Holy Bible in the book of Genesis, we see this entire structure of the mind outlined in full detail. The creation story is not an origin story of mankind, it is the depiction of the creation of the tools and vehicles for our consciousness to experience.

Genesis 1:1-3

God created the heavens and the Earth in the very beginning. And the Earth was without form, and void; and darkness was upon the face of the deep. And the Spirit of God moved upon the face of the water. And God said 'let there be light;' and there was light.

UNIVERSAL LANGUAGE OF THE MIND

HEAVEN = Superconscious mind
EARTH = Subconscious mind
GOD = The Most High
LORD = Real Self
TIME = Evolution of Consciousness
DARKNESS = Unawareness
FACE = Identity
LIGHT = Awareness
SPIRIT = Breath
WATER = Life experience

The first word in the bible is God. You will notice as you read through the bible that sometimes the term 'God' is used and at other times 'the Lord' is used. Many people pay no mind to when one is used versus the other and only perceive them as interchangeable. However, there is a difference between the two and there is a purpose and intent behind when one is used rather than the other. When you see the word 'God' used in the bible it is referring to the light of the creator. When you come across the term 'the Lord' it is referring to your IAM divine consciousness, your Real Self. We immediately see that the creation story and the bible begin with God because OUR creation and existence begins and originates with the essence of the Most High.

'God created the heavens and the earth in the very beginning'

Time in the Universal Language of the Mind is not linear as we see it within this physical reality. It is vertical and a representation of the evolution of our consciousness. The beginning represents the initiation of our consciousness into the movement into mind. The first thing created was the mind; the heavens and the Earth.

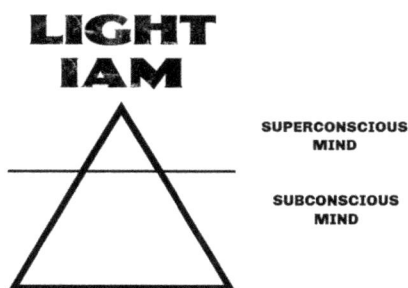

**LIGHT
IAM**

SUPERCONSCIOUS
MIND

SUBCONSCIOUS
MIND

In the Universal Language of the Mind the heavens, or the sky, have always represented the superconscious mind. In every holy scripture the Earth has always represented the subconscious mind.

'And the earth was without form, and void'

As our consciousness first moved into the field of experience there was an emptiness as nothing had yet been manifested. There are no experiences yet had within the superconscious mind or the subconscious mind. The purpose of this movement of consciousness into the spirit, soul, and body, into the superconscious mind, subconscious mind, and conscious mind is to have experiences in order to know and understand our True Selves.

'And darkness was upon the face of the deep'

This is indicating the unawareness of who we are. Faces in the Universal Language of the mind represents identity. We have our faces on our ID, we use faces in order to identify our friends and family and those we know. Many of us can reflect upon a time when we saw someone we thought we knew until they turned around and we realized it was not them the moment we were able to see their face. The deep is indicating that there is space. The possibilities of our existence and experience is not shallow but is very deep.

'And the spirit of God moved upon the face of the water'

The word spirit means breath. Our breath is the carrier of our lifeforce energy. The prana encapsulated within the oxygen molecules that we breathe in are the source of our life. This lifeforce energy is needed for life to exist and is needed to feed into any creation. We are creators. Our life force energy is the source of our creative power. This verse is conveying out power to create our life experiences in order to identify who we truly are. The face of the water represents the entire field of experience within the mind, the triangle.

And God said 'let there be light;' and there was light.

When we first moved into the field of experience there was nothing there, it was empty, and we were unaware. Just by entering we have now initiated new experience and the first thing created is awareness. The key here is to focus upon HOW God created. You will notice that every time something is manifested it was due to an invocation by the creator. God SAID... The spoken word holds power in creation. The words you choose to speak hold power. Be mindful and aware of the words you invoke as they reverberate out into our reality and have an effect on all of existence.

Genesis 1:4-5

And God saw that the light was good; and God separated the light from the darkness. And God called the light day and the darkness he called night. And there was evening and there was morning, the first day.

UNIVERSAL LANGUAGE OF THE MIND

SIGHT = Perception
LIGHT = Awareness
DARKNESS = Unawareness
TIME = Evolution of Consciousness
ONE = Individuality

Now that awareness has been created we can identify and perceive the difference between being aware of something and being unaware of something. In perceiving our increasing awareness of our self we can identify that it is a good thing and that we can benefit from it. To be good is to have purpose, to be productive, and to generate growth.

The separation of the light and darkness is the awareness of moving from the Light of the Creator which is the Source of our existence and moving out into this deep space and void of unawareness within the mind.

**LIGHT
IAM**

The completion of the '*first day*' is a completion of one cycle of growth. Life is all about circles or cycles. As we move and progress through life we will either learn from what we experience and elevate our consciousness or we will need to recreate new opportunities to learn in future experiences.

If we continue to learn, then we will continue to spiral upwards as we progress further and further into understanding Self, creation, and the universe. If we continue to refuse to learn then we will circle back around to the same type of experiences over and over until we finally choose to learn from the opportunities made available to us.

The number one represents individuality. We have now fully embarked on the beginning of the journey to know the Self. This is initiating our awareness of our own individuality.

Genesis 1:6-8

*And God said let there be a firmament
in the midst of the waters, and let it
divide the waters from the waters.
And God made the firmament, and
divided the waters that were under
the firmament from the waters that
were above the firmament. And God
called the firmament sky. And there
was evening and there was morning,
the second day*

UNIVERSAL LANGUAGE OF THE MIND

-MENT = Mind
WATER = Life experience
SKY = Superconscious mind
2 = Duality

The etymology of the suffix '*-ment*'
means mind. *Govern-ment* represents the
governing of minds. *Ail-ment* is a reflection
of the unproductive thoughts within the
mind that produce dis-ease and dis-order.
En-light-en-ment reflects the increased light
within the mind. Light = awareness, thus

we can see that enlightenment truly means increased awareness within the mind.

The *'firm-a-ment'* represents the foundation of the mind that provides support for the framework of the structure of our mind. The superconscious mind holds the blueprint for our existence. The first level into the subconscious mind is the mental level. As the energy of the idea of our blueprint moves from the superconscious mind and crosses over into the subconscious mind it becomes more real, it gets more firm as it forms into a thought within the mental level.

'And God said let there be a firmament in the midst of the waters, and let it divide the waters from the waters. And God made the firmament, and divided the waters that were under the firmament from the waters that were above the firmament.'

The waters represents the field of experience which is the whole mind. The foundational structure is the firmament which is providing a more solid form and firmness to the mind. It is placed within the mind, in the midst. We now see that there is a separation between the two. An indication of difference to be made. The superconscious mind above the firmament is whole amongst itself. The space in mind below the firmament is whole amongst itself.

The number two represents duality. On the second day this duality was created. There are now two levels of experience that each have their own way of fulfilling the purpose of knowing the Self and understanding who we are.

Genesis 1:9-10

*And God said, let the waters that are
under the sky be gathered together in
one place, and let the dry land
appear; and it was so, And God called
the dry land Earth; and the gathering
together of the waters He called seas;
and God saw that it was good.*

UNIVERSAL LANGUAGE OF THE MIND

WATER = Life experience
SKY = Superconscious mind
LAND/EARTH = Subconscious Mind
SEAS = Conscious mind

'And God Said...'

Once again God has invoked words in
order to create something. Nothing has
been created yet without God first invoking
it.

**LIGHT
IAM**

SUPERCONSCIOUS
MIND

SUBCONSCIOUS
MIND

CONSCIOUS MIND

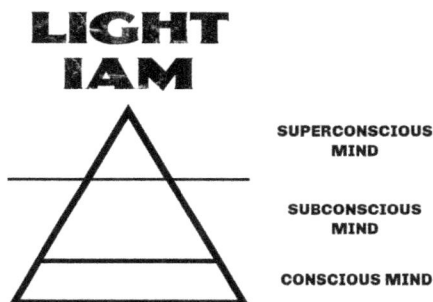

'...let the waters that are under the sky be gathered into one place, and let the dry land appear;'

Another separation has been created. The separation between land and water. The land is the subconscious mind and the water gathered together represents our life experiences within the conscious mind, within this physical reality.

'...And it was so'

There is nothing more needed to manifest. The invocation of a thought is all that is needed and it will be so. The speed in which it manifests will be determined by your will power. If you invoke a singular thought, unwavering, with purpose, it will be sure to manifest just as you have commanded it to.

Isaiah 55:11

'So shall My word be that goes forth from My mouth; it shall not return to me void....'

Every thought seeks to manifest. The energy you feed into the thought forms within your mind will always set out to produce something. Those thoughts that you choose to invoke and speak out loud will have even more energy behind them. That energy will not return empty handed, something will be produced from it.

Isaiah 55:11

'... But it WILL accomplish what I please, and it WILL prosper in the thin for which I sent it'

The strength of your will power ensures that what you have intended with your invocation of your thoughts is manifested exactly as it was imaged. Your will power is the deciding factor on how instantaneous the universe responds in that manifestation.

This is why concentration and will power are so vital to our spiritual development. We are powerful manifestors. The Universal Law of Cause and Effect is at work at all times for everyone. Your thoughts create your reality and every thought seeks to manifest. The stronger your concentration, the better you will be at holding in mind the thoughts that you desire to see manifested. The stronger your will power, the more energy you can feed into those thought forms ensuring what you desire is what becomes manifest.

When distractions arise within the mind we experience delays in what we desire or we see manifested things and experiences that we never desired in the first place. A distraction could be doubting ourselves or not believing in ourselves. A distraction could be a negative thought or an unproductive belief. Any thought or idea that does not align with your desired image is a distraction.

When we become distracted we feed energy into that thought form instead of our desired goal. When we become distracted we must use our concentration, our ability to control our attention, to redirect our focus back onto what we truly desire and then use our will power to hold it there. The KEYS 2 SUCCESS course is designed to guide you on how to strengthen both your concentration and your will power. I would highly suggest that you begin working on both immediately.

CONCLUSION

There have been a lot of beautiful gems presented within this book. We have unearthed many ancient metaphysical concepts. However, none of this information holds an ounce of value to you without experience. Without creating further experiences for yourself in order to discover the truths laid out here for yourself then everything here is just more information.

Information will not transform your life. Concepts will not produce a change within you and elevate your consciousness. Be sure to produce experiences for yourself in order to transform this information into your own knowledge. Continue to deepen your awareness of self.

Begin recording your dreams to examine in deeper ways your existence within your subconscious mind. Perform daily the memory, attention, and imagination exercises within chapter 4 to strengthen the power of your conscious mind. Go deeper with your prayer and once complete spend time listering for a response in order to connect more with your superconscious mind. Practice many different conscious breathing techniques in order to align with your spirit. Read my first book and take the DREAM INTERPRETATION MASTERCLASS to become fluent in the Universal Language of the Mind in order to decode your dreams and decipher holy scriptures. Observe and examine your thoughts as they enter your mind.

Whatever it is that you decide to do with your life, be sure to have a purpose for it. If you have not discovered what your purpose is, then generate a meaningful purpose to move forward with until you do.

Create an intention for each day that you wake up in and every activity that you experience. Spend time each day reflecting on what you have the opportunity to learn based upon what you have experienced, are experiencing, and will be experiencing.

As you fall asleep every night, activate your imagination and play out the movie of the life you want your future self to live and spare no detail. The moment you ever find yourself imagining or entertaining a thought of something you do not wish to experience then burn that image up in a wall of flames. Then take the energy within the ashes to form a moving image of what it is that you do want to experience.

Read the Tao Te Ching. Read the Dhammapada. Read the Yogi Sutras of Patanjali. Read the Book of Secrets. Read the Bhagavad Gita. Read the Gospel of Zarathustra. Read the Upanishads. Use these scriptures to elevate your perspective. Once you learn the Universal Language of the Mind, go and read the Book of Matthew and the Book of Revelations within the Bible.

This is your life. You are free to do whatever you choose. This is the Universal Law of the Divine Birthright. However, I will always encourage you to do things that are intended to aid you in your soul growth and spiritual development. And if you are someone who is interested in accelerating your spiritual evolution then join the Metaphysical Mentorship today.

PEACE.